BUSINE
FOR T
PEOPL

BCS, THE CHARTERED INSTITUTE FOR IT

BCS, The Chartered Institute for IT, champions the global IT profession and the interests of individuals engaged in that profession for the benefit of all. We promote wider social and economic progress through the advancement of information technology science and practice. We bring together industry, academics, practitioners and government to share knowledge, promote new thinking, inform the design of new curricula, shape public policy and inform the public.

Our vision is to be a world-class organisation for IT. Our 70,000 strong membership includes practitioners, businesses, academics and students in the UK and internationally. We deliver a range of professional development tools for practitioners and employees. A leading IT qualification body, we offer a range of widely recognised qualifications.

Further Information
BCS, The Chartered Institute for IT,
First Floor, Block D,
North Star House, North Star Avenue,
Swindon, SN2 1FA, United Kingdom.
T +44 (0) 1793 417 424
F +44 (0) 1793 417 444
www.bcs.org/contact

http://shop.bcs.org/

BUSINESS WRITING FOR TECHNICAL PEOPLE
The most effective ways to get your message across

Carrie Marshall

Published by BCS Learning & Development Ltd, a wholly owned subsidiary of BCS, The Chartered Institute for IT, First Floor, Block D, North Star House, North Star Avenue, Swindon, SN2 1FA, UK. www.bcs.org

Paperback ISBN: 978-1-78017-4457
PDF ISBN: 978-1-78017-4426
ePUB ISBN: 978-1-78017-4433
Kindle ISBN: 978-1-78017-4440

Ebook available

British Cataloguing in Publication Data.
A CIP catalogue record for this book is available at the British Library.

Disclaimer:
The views expressed in this book are of the author and do not necessarily reflect the views of the Institute or BCS Learning & Development Ltd except where explicitly stated as such. Although every care has been taken by the author and BCS Learning & Development Ltd in the preparation of the publication, no warranty is given by the authors or BCS Learning & Development Ltd as publisher as to the accuracy or completeness of the information contained within it and neither the authors nor BCS Learning & Development Ltd shall be responsible or liable for any loss or damage whatsoever arising by virtue of such information or any instructions or advice contained within this publication or by any of the aforementioned.

BCS books are available at special quantity discounts to use as premiums and sale promotions, or for use in corporate training programmes. Please visit our Contact Us page at www.bcs.org/contact

Publisher's acknowledgements
Reviewers: Oliver Lindberg and Justin Richards
Publisher: Ian Borthwick
Commissioning Editor: Rebecca Youé
Production Manager: Florence Leroy
Project Manager: Sunrise Setting Ltd
Cover work: Alex Wright
Picture credits: Shutterstock/DenisProduction.com
Typeset by Lapiz Digital Services, Chennai, India.
Printed by Hobbs the Printers Ltd, Totton, Hampshire, SO40 3WX

CONTENTS

ABOUT THE AUTHOR

Carrie Marshall is a journalist, copywriter, ghostwriter and broadcaster from Glasgow. A professional writer for 20 years, she has written thousands of features, columns, reviews and news stories for a huge range of magazines, newspapers, websites and trade publications. As a copywriter she has crafted copy for some of the biggest names in the technology, retail, audio and finance industries, and as a novelist she sold enough copies of her self-published debut to buy a car. Not a great car, but still a car! Under various names, Carrie has written 11 non-fiction books, co-written six more and co-written a six-part Radio 2 documentary series. She blogs at www.bigmouthstrikesagain.com and tweets as @carrieinglasgow.

PREFACE

This book is for people who know their stuff.

It's for the programmers and the engineers, the product managers and the analysts, the people who know how things work and how to get things done.

It's all about communicating what you know to the people who need to know it, and how to do that in the easiest, simplest and best way.

In this book you will discover how to communicate in the most effective way, the resources you will need to get the job done and the tricks that can transform even the most daunting document.

In Chapter 1 you'll explore what business writing really means, and why bad writing is bad news for everybody.

In Chapter 2 you'll find out how to learn the tricks of the trade by reading other people's words.

In Chapter 3 you'll discover why good business writing is simply about telling a story.

Chapter 4 explains the differences in writing for different kinds of people, and for different kinds of publications.

In Chapter 5 we'll take our writing to the gym and make it leaner.

Chapter 6 explores the dangers of jargon, and how clear language makes all the difference to effective communication.

Chapter 7 is your survival guide to making a business case for an investment or other important business change.

In Chapter 8 you'll discover how to write well for the internet, and to ensure that Google likes what you do.

Chapter 9 focuses on the importance of editing and testing your work.

In Chapter 10 you'll learn how to deal with the kind of writing everybody dreads: communicating bad news.

Chapter 11 gives you the tools to deal with the dreaded writer's block, and what to do if the words don't come.

And in Chapter 12 you can laugh at other people's mistakes in the Business Writing House of Horrors.

1 WHAT IS BUSINESS WRITING?

Business writing is something we all do without necessarily thinking about it. It's the writing we do as part of our day-to-day work: emails, memos, proposals, reports and anything else we use to communicate with our colleagues, clients or customers.

Good business writing matters. We spend a great deal of our working time reading, so waffly writing is a waste of that time. Vague communications don't inspire trust from colleagues or clients. Proposals that are not persuasive won't get the green light. Brochures full of buzzwords will leave potential customers cold.

Unfortunately, a lot of the business writing we all receive isn't as good as it should be. Our inboxes overflow with jargon-heavy reports, emails that take forever to get to the point and memos that need to be read four times to work out what on Earth the writer is on about.

It doesn't have to be that way.

WHY BAD WRITING IS BAD NEWS

Bad writing is bad for productivity. When *Harvard Business Review* surveyed 547 business people about their reading habits, it found that they averaged 25.5 hours per week reading at work. That was mostly email. Eight-one per cent of them said that bad writing was a massive waste of their time, because email was often 'too long, poorly organised, unclear, filled with jargon and imprecise' (Bernoff, 2016). The senders might as well have sent pictures of bears wearing top hats. At least that would be funny.

Business writing gets a bad rap because so much of it is awful. Sometimes that's deliberate, the corporate equivalent of a politician refusing to answer a straight question. But often it's because people simply haven't been given the tools to do it properly.

You wouldn't sit somebody down in front of a PC and expect them to write code without any training or experience, yet every day businesses do just that with business writing. Just because somebody's an expert in their field doesn't mean they have been given the tools they need to communicate their expertise and enthusiasm in the best possible way.

That's what this book is here for.

2 LEARNING TO WRITE WITHOUT FEAR

Some people say that writing is an art, something that requires God-given talent. Those people are professional writers who don't want anybody to know how easy their job is. The truth is that good writing is a craft. Anybody can do it and, like any craft, the more you do it the better you get.

When you consider how important business writing is to any organisation, the fact that most firms don't teach it is incredible; especially when the secrets of successful business writing are actually very simple.

In this chapter you will discover how a little bit of preparation and a little bit of reading can help give you the confidence you need to write effectively and without fear.

TAKE YOUR TIME

The most important thing in business writing isn't talent. It's time. Time to think about what you are going to write, time to do any research and collate any necessary resources, time to write and then time to edit the writing to make it better.

It's also important to have time to read. The more you read, the more of other people's writing you can look at with a critical eye, the better your own writing will become.

Your eyes will begin to glaze over when confronted with something like this:

> As the pace of accomplishments continues to accelerate, proof-point has become a necessity. Cross-pollination and market practice digitize our agility resulting in a measured efficiency gain; this is why there can be no productivity improvement until we can achieve a sustained increase in margins.

That's from a website called the Corporate Bullshit Generator,[1] which automatically generates streams of convincing-sounding nonsense from real buzzwords and phrases. We receive genuine documents and emails exactly like that every day. Beware the added-value solutions provider, the game changer, the establishment of a new paradigm in customer facing solutions leveraging location specific core competencies.

If you have ever been shopping for a new car you'll know how the cars you're considering are suddenly everywhere: every second car seems to be a Ford Mondeo, an Audi A5 or a Mercedes E220. It's the same with meaningless business jargon. Once you start noticing it, you see it everywhere – and you start to notice if you're falling into the same traps.

BORROW BRIGHT IDEAS

It's important to look for good writing as well as bad. Good business writing gets to the point, gets a message across clearly and, if appropriate, has a personality too.

Here is the 'About Us' intro from Linn,[2] maker of high-tech home audio products:

> Music makes life better.

> It's the sound of your greatest achievements and happiest moments. It's the soundtrack to the best of times with the people you love the most. It's a source of energy and inspiration, of comfort and of joy.

> It's beautiful. Powerful. Magical. And we make it better.

---

[1] See https://cbsg.sf.net
[2] See https://www.linn.co.uk/about

I'll admit to a bit of bias, because I wrote that one, but hopefully you'll agree that the writing does its job without going over the top: you immediately know what Linn is all about.

Here is the online project management service, Trello's,[3] board basics:

The Basics

Let's go over some board basics. A new Trello board is like a clean slate, ready to organise any of your life's projects.

A board represents a project. Whether you are redesigning a kitchen or launching a new website, a Trello board is the place to organise your tasks on lists and collaborate with your team of friends, family and colleagues.

That's very good business writing: it's clear, jargon-free and tells you exactly what you need to know.

And here is Apple,[4] trying to sell you an iPhone 8:

iPhone 8 introduces an all-new glass design. The world's most popular camera, now even better. The smartest, most powerful chip ever in an iPhone. Wireless charging that's truly effortless. And augmented reality experiences never before possible. iPhone 8. A new generation of iPhone.

These are all marketing communications: Linn's is about communicating a brand identity; Trello's is explaining how you would use its service; Apple is trying to get you to buy a £800 phone. And you can learn from them because any kind of business writing is a form of selling.

You might be trying to sell an idea rather than a product, but the purpose is usually to persuade the recipient to do, say or agree with something. That doesn't mean you should make

---

[3] See https://trello.com/guide/board-basics.html
[4] See https://www.apple.com/uk/iphone-8/

your work emails read like iPhone adverts, but you can make them more effective by learning some of the same tricks the commercial copywriters have used.

KEY TAKEAWAYS

- Writing is a craft. The more you do it, the better you get.
- Good business writing gets to the point and communicates clearly.
- Give yourself time not just to write, but to read others' writing.

3 THINK BEFORE YOU INK

There's an old marketing saying: sell the sizzle, not the sausage. We buy sausages not because of what's in them – for many of us that's something we would rather not think about – but because of how we think they will taste. What matters is the benefit, not the ingredients.

Effective business communication does the same thing. It doesn't have to be selling a product: it could be an idea, or a proposal. But it's the sizzle that you need to think about before you start writing.

In this chapter you will discover the difference between describing what something does, and what it can do for the person you're describing it to.

SELLING THE SIZZLE: AN IT EXAMPLE

Let's return to Apple's iPhone sales page. In many ways Apple are masters of corporate communication, especially when it comes to writing sparkling copy. Here are some more bits from the iPhone 8 page.

The glass back enables easy wireless charging.

True Tone technology automatically adjusts white balance to match the light around you. For a better viewing experience in all kinds of environments.

With a wide colour gamut and our best colour accuracy ever, everything on the screen looks more brilliant and vibrant.

iOS 11 is our most advanced, intuitive and secure mobile operating system yet. It's designed to help you get the most out of iPhone.

Get to apps in Messages with fewer taps. Let Siri be your personal DJ. And discover new music with friends in Apple Music.

Have you spotted it? Each time Apple describes a particular feature it does so by saying what it can do for you. Easy charging. Matching the light around you. Helping you get the most from your phone. It's selling the sizzle, not the sausage. The glass back is undoubtedly pretty and a great bit of engineering, but it's there to make your day that little bit easier and that's what Apple emphasises.

What Apple is doing here is selling a story. In this case, the story is that you should buy a phone and it will make your life better. Your story may be that investing in IT infrastructure will make the business more efficient, or it may be that a firm who uses your service will become more flexible than a circus contortionist.

When you're telling your story, it's important that you put yourself in the reader's shoes. A product getting a new feature isn't an interesting story, no matter how important or clever that feature may be. It's what that feature can do for the reader that matters.

Let's take a really simple example: the battery in a smartphone. If you're technically minded, you'll know that a phone battery with capacity of 3,750 mAh is a big improvement over one with 3,000 mAh, but to the average person those numbers are meaningless unless you translate them into something they care about. An extra 750 mAh of battery capacity isn't interesting to most of us. A phone that doesn't run out of puff, even on the most demanding days, is.

If you don't know what your story is, then anything you write is a joke without a punchline, a thriller that doesn't thrill, a band that noodles around on stage for what seems like hours when the audience only wants to hear the hits. The story is the message you are trying to send, and if you don't know what it is then it's impossible to communicate it clearly.

In most cases, the message you're trying to communicate is the same:

If you do this, your life will be better.

'This' may be buying a product, subscribing to a service or not getting into trouble by using work PCs for personal shopping. It might be a huge investment in infrastructure or a change to the way things are done in a particular department, or 'better' could be something solid such as increased profits, something less tangible such as improved employee morale, or just the avoidance of disciplinary action if your daytime eBay habit is discovered.

Here are some examples of stories you might want to share:

- If we spend X on Y, we'll save Z.

- We're not the cheapest, but our product does more useful things than our rivals.

- If you buy this product, your working day will be easier.

- Switching from their service to our service will save you huge piles of money.

- Moving to new premises will be a hassle, but it's a better location and the canteen's brilliant.

- This job has your name on it.

- Once we've had a bit of training, the new system will get rid of that thing that everybody hates so much.

- You already know we're brilliant at this, but did you know we're the best at that too, so we can help you even more?

LIGHTS, EMAIL, ACTION!

In addition to knowing the story you want to tell, you also need to decide what you want the result of your communication to be. That's where the 'call to action' comes in.

The call to action (CTA for short) is the bit of the document, email or social media post that asks the reader to do something. You might want them to click on a link to a product page, or to fill out a form for more information. You might be soliciting feedback about a new system that's being tested. You might just want to stop people nicking your milk from the communal fridge. Whatever it is, it should be clear what the next step should be before you start writing, because the whole point is to get the reader to take the action you want them to take.

If you can't think of what you want your writing to achieve, it's worth taking a step back and asking whether the thing you plan to write is actually necessary. If it isn't, don't write it. You've just saved yourself and your readers a whole bunch of time and made the world a slightly better place.

KEY TAKEAWAYS

- Sell the sizzle, not the sausage.
- Effective writing shares a story.
- Establish what you want your writing to achieve.

4 CHOOSE YOUR WEAPONS

Writing is rarely a one-size-fits-all activity. You need to write differently for different audiences, and you may need to write differently depending on where your message will be read. For example, Twitter tweets, Facebook posts and a lot of emails are read by people when they are travelling or just quickly picking up their phone, so you need to get to the point quickly. In some cases, you might need to write the same thing multiple times in different ways for different audiences.

In this chapter you will learn the key things to consider when you're writing for different audiences, or different sectors of the same audience.

KNOW YOUR AUDIENCE

As different people need to be communicated with in different ways, the first question to ask yourself is the most important one: Who am I writing this for?

Someone who gets pitched IT projects all day every day will have an exceptionally short attention span and zero tolerance for hype, whereas a director considering an expensive IT investment will want detailed research and solid financial projections. A small team will be happy with informal language, but such language might be inappropriate if sent company-wide.

There are cultural differences too. If you're communicating with people from different parts of the world or with differing cultures, there may be specific things you'll need to explain, or comparisons or concepts that won't translate from one language or culture to another.

There is also the generation gap to consider. Something that's obvious to you might not be obvious to somebody older or younger. You and I might remember when Microsoft Windows came with a huge bunch of floppy disks, but many people using computers today think floppy disks are 3D-printed 'Save' icons because they grew up long after floppies became obsolete.

Another key issue is the readers' level of knowledge. Terms and acronyms that experts in a particular industry use every day might not mean anything to other employees, so there's a danger of coming across like the car mechanic who says a whole bunch of things you don't understand, but which clearly mean you're going to make a big dent in your bank account.

Effective communication is all about getting your message across as clearly as possible, and that means speaking the right language.

Speaking the *right* language doesn't necessarily mean speaking the *same* language. A 40-something manager attempting to write in the language his or her teenage employees might use socially is heading into embarrassing-parent territory, and such attempts can seem patronising even when you get the language right.

Speaking the right language means using language that is clear, appropriate and gets your message across without any confusion or anybody having to Google the terms you use.

PICK YOUR PLATFORM

Once you've identified the audience, the next step is to think about where that audience will read your message. Will it be an email they'll receive while fielding constant calls from customers? Will it be something they'll read in detail first thing when they come to work, or a social media post they'll glance at on their morning commute?

There are practical limitations too. Twitter currently gives you 280 characters for a tweet, and chains of tweets on a single topic are frowned upon. Figure 4.1 shows a tweet from the BCS Twitter account.

Figure 4.1 A tweet from the BCS Twitter account. Tailor your message to the platform; for example, Twitter is all about brevity.

Email doesn't have that limit, but the recipient's time may be precious, so a descriptive email subject and a lack of waffle will help get your message across. A similar approach works well with posts on the business network LinkedIn too.

HOPE FOR THE BEST AND PLAN FOR THE WORST

While it's crucial to know who you're writing for, it's also worth considering where your message might end up – especially if you're writing something with sensitive content that could be taken out of context or is written in a way that might offend somebody.

The internet is often an instant outrage machine where perfectly well-meaning words are misinterpreted and widely circulated.

It's always better to try and prevent such misinterpretation than to try and deal with a publicity nightmare. As Jonathan Swift wrote, way back in 1710: 'Falsehood flies, and the truth comes limping after it.'[5]

That doesn't mean you shouldn't write with personality or humour, but it's worth asking: What's the worst possible way somebody could interpret this? Humour, especially sarcastic British humour, often doesn't translate very well; the only humour that's almost guaranteed to work anywhere in the world is physical comedy.

Humour isn't the only concern. There are countless examples of companies getting into trouble because of unconscious bias, lack of thought or good old-fashioned bad luck. Sometimes they manage to combine all three.

Even very simple bits of writing can cause offence, often because people didn't assume the worst; for example, Facebook recently caused great offence with its apparently harmless feature showing people the most-liked things they had ever posted. Unfortunately, Facebook didn't consider that, for some people, the most liked and most commented posts were the ones announcing serious personal trauma or the death of relatives. The cheerful copy didn't fit well with photos of funerals.

Sara Wachter-Boettcher's book, *Technically Wrong* (Wachter-Boettcher, 2017), provides multiple examples of such PR disasters, including sexist chatbots, online forms that accidentally offend LGBT people and assumptions that make algorithms behave in apparently biased ways. Also recommended are Wachter-Boettcher's book with Eric Meyer about inclusivity, *Design for Real Life* (2016), and *Tragic Design* by Jonathan Shariat and Cynthia Savard Saucier (2016) (www.tragicdesign.com). Together, these books demonstrate not only how easy it is to get it wrong, but how easy it is to get it right.

---

[5] In his essay 'Political Lying', available at: www.bartleby.com/209/633.html

TAKE A PICTURE

Sometimes the clearest way to express something is to use a picture. We are all familiar with organisation charts, flow charts and graphs, and wisely chosen images can be more effective than giant blocks of text. 'Wisely chosen' is the important bit. If you've ever dozed through a bad PowerPoint presentation, you'll know that, while a picture can paint a thousand words, a slideshow can feel like a thousand years.

One of the most useful kinds of business graphic is the infographic, which is an attractively designed image that provides information in a punchy way. Figure 4.2 is an example of an infographic (only shown in part, for brevity).

Writing an infographic is rather like writing an advert. The key features are:

i.   a short, snappy headline;
ii. a short and interesting introduction;
iii. some eye-catching numbers and/or graphs;
iv. very short explanations for each section.

With infographics, less is more: if you've written lots of paragraphs, your graphic is probably too densely packed to be effective. An infographic should work like a poster: you must be able to understand what it's saying almost immediately. And, like a poster, it needs to have a good design to be effective. If design isn't one of your skills, rope in someone to do your words justice.

KEY TAKEAWAYS

- Different people need to be written to in different ways.
- Use language that's clear and appropriate for your readers.
- Humour doesn't always translate very well.

Figure 4.2 Part of an infographic about Bill Gates from Frugaldad.com (used with permission).

5 FIGHT THE FLAB

In this chapter you will learn how to take your writing to the gym and make it leaner and punchier.

One magazine editor I spoke to shared a top tip: when you've written something, go back and delete the first paragraph. Nine times out of ten, the piece works better without it (yes, I deleted the first paragraph of this chapter).

That's a good example of business writing's biggest enemy: flab. Flab is the stuff your piece doesn't need, and it often slips in as the result of habits picked up over the years.

One way to fight the flab in business writing is to take the same approach professional writers do when they write press releases. Press releases – good ones, anyway – are written like a pyramid, with the punchiest bit at the very top and the most detailed bits at the very bottom. They'll start with a short, sharp, interesting headline and then they'll summarise the whole story in an interesting way in a sentence or two. After that, they'll add more detail.

Writers do that because many editors simply won't read beyond that point: they're too busy to read every press release in detail. Business writing is aimed at very busy people too, so make sure the key information is communicated quickly and effectively at the very beginning.

Here are the most common forms of flab to look for and banish from your business writing.

UNNECESSARY EXPERTISE

You're the expert, and your brain is full of valuable information, but do you need to share it all in this particular piece of writing?

Let's take a real example of business writing from the world of IT training. I was asked to deliver an introductory course for absolute beginners – and by beginners I mean people who didn't know whether the mouse sits on the desk, goes in front of the screen or sits on the floor like a piano pedal – and the training materials began with the history of the IBM PC and how the really important player in the development of the PC clone business wasn't IBM, but Compaq.

That's mildly interesting to those of us who care about computing's history, but it's completely irrelevant for a practical training course. It's like being expected to study the history of the internal combustion engine before the car dealer lets you choose your new car.

It's easy to fall into the trap of providing too much information. It's natural that we want people to understand things. But more often than not, people don't need to understand the background to what you're showing them.

If you're providing a lot of background information, it's worth channelling your inner teenager and asking: Who cares?

THE PASSIVE VOICE AND WEAK VERBS

You might not be familiar with the term – although Microsoft Office's grammar checker really hates the passive voice and says so frequently – but you're probably familiar with the boredom the passive voice creates. It's when writing is unnecessarily distant and stilted and uses weak or 'passive' verbs to describe something; so, for example, somebody would write:

It was decided that ...

when it's much better to say:

We decided ...

The active voice is more direct and tells you who and what, in that order. For example, instead of:

It has been noted that some employees have been using their work PCs for personal browsing.

it would be better to say:

Employees have been using their work PCs for personal browsing.

Better still:

Don't use work PCs for personal browsing.

Here's another. Instead of:

Our product has been imitated by our competitor.

it's punchier to say:

Our competitor copied our product.

This sentence is weak:

I used my skills to contribute to improving the company's website.

and this is strong:

I redesigned the company's website.

This is okay:

I was in charge of ...

but this is better:

I managed ...

This isn't necessarily wrong:

> The ticket can then be escalated to second line support.

but this is simpler:

> Refer the case to second line support.

You've probably seen something like this:

> Employees are not permitted to ...

but this does the same job:

> Please don't ...

The difference isn't always dramatic, but effective business writing is all about getting the maximum effect from your words. Avoiding the passive voice helps with that.

TOO MANY WORDS

As the excellent guidebook, *The Elements of Style*, by William Strunk and E.B. White puts it (1999):

> A sentence should contain no unnecessary words, a paragraph no unnecessary sentences, for the same reason that a drawing should have no unnecessary lines and a machine no unnecessary parts.

LONG SENTENCES AND ENDLESS PARAGRAPHS

There's a reason marketing copy is usually short. It's because brevity works. Short and snappy can be very effective.

For best results though, it's a good idea to mix things up, especially with longer pieces where too much brevity becomes tiresome.

Sometimes, it's worth emphasising things by starting a new paragraph.

When you're writing, take a look at it in full page view. Is it a forbidding rectangular block of words with precious little white space and sentences that go on forever, adding lots of words to the original point without actually doing anything constructive, resulting in something that if you were to read out in one breath would have you keeling over because it takes so long to read that you would run out of oxygen long before you reached the second-last comma, which came before another bunch of words that did absolutely nothing of any use whatsoever?

You get the point, I'm sure.

SHOWING OFF

Some people have wonderful vocabularies, especially when it comes to the specific areas they're experts in. But good writing isn't about showing off how much you know. It's about communicating clearly. Using 'discombobulated' when you could say 'confused', or using an acronym your readers won't know, isn't helping anybody.

CLICHÉS

At the end of the day, it is what it is. We need to take things to the next level, think outside the box, touch base with our key stakeholders 24/7 and hit the ground running. It's a win–win situation, a no-brainer, and we don't need to reinvent the wheel provided we give it 110 per cent. Let's run it up the flagpole and see who salutes.

Clichés, especially clichés like the ones above, use a lot of letters to say very little. They're generally used by scoundrels.

WOOLLY WRITING

Woolly is another way of saying vague, confused or lacking in clarity. When writing is woolly, it's often because the person who wrote it didn't go through the steps identified earlier: knowing what story you want to tell; knowing what you want your readers to do; and knowing where and how to address the people you want to communicate with.

One way to avoid woolly writing is to plan what you are going to write in the form of bulleted or numbered lists. That's what I did as I wrote this book: I decided what chapters to have, and then what things I was going to cover in each chapter.

For example, my plan for this chapter looked like this:

Ch. 5 – flab

1. What's flab?
    1.1 Expertise
    1.2 Passive voice (examples)
    1.3 Too many words
    1.4 Long sentences
    1.5 Clichés
    1.6 Woolly writing
    1.7 Orwell

It's a great way to keep you focused and to stop you wandering off on tangents.

Another form of woolly writing is to use vague terms for things that can be measured and quantified: time; or money; or anything else you can count. Descriptive terms such as 'a little while' are fine for casual writing or conversational copywriting, but any document that needs clarity, such as an instruction manual, proposal or procedure, should be clear when it comes to quantities. Think of it like a recipe: if the cook doesn't use the right ingredients in the right quantities, they probably won't get the right results.

TAKE ADVICE FROM GEORGE ORWELL

The journalist and novelist George Orwell's essay 'Politics and the English Language' contains some of the best writing advice you'll ever read. He wrote it in 1946, but it's just as relevant today.

His key advice was that you should think about what you're trying to say. Are you saying it as well as you can, without waffling or vagueness? Is there anything 'avoidably ugly' that you should change (Orwell, 1946)?

Orwell's advice can be summed up in just one word: simplify. Use fewer, shorter words, avoid foreign words or jargon, and always try to make your writing leaner. But I like his final tip the best:

> Break any of these rules sooner than say anything barbarous.

KEY TAKEAWAYS

- Nobody ever wished a memo, report or presentation was longer.
- Be ruthless: get rid of anything your writing doesn't need.
- Use active words, not the passive tense.

6   JUNK THE JARGON

Whether it's IT or the army, cloud computing or the charity sector, every industry has its own language. That language is often completely baffling to outsiders, but it's a useful shortcut for insiders.

In this chapter you will discover when jargon can help speed up communication, and when it actually makes communication more difficult. You will also discover why buzzwords are best avoided.

WHAT IS JARGON?

Jargon is language that's specific to a particular group or profession, and is often expressed as acronyms. It serves a useful purpose: used correctly, it enables people to communicate more efficiently with each other.

Surgeons use medical jargon to communicate with their surgical team (and in some cases to avoid alarming the patient). Shops famously use code words to alert staff to unpleasantness in the aisles or bathrooms.

IT suppliers use jargon to describe particular products, services or concepts – the Internet of Things (IoT), for example, or Software as a Service (SaaS), or Cascading Style Sheets (CSS; used for website design).

The Ministry of Defence (MoD) is particularly keen on acronyms. If you go to the www.gov.uk website you can find a helpful list of MoD acronyms from 1ACC (Number one Air Control Centre) to ZZ (Zig-Zag), covering essential terms such as 2SL/CNH (Second Sea Lord Commander in Chief Naval Home Command).

The MoD list is 373 pages long.

Doctors use terms such as BMI (body mass index), NSAID (non-steroidal anti-inflammatory drugs), BP (blood pressure) and LDL (low density lipoproteins, aka 'bad' cholesterol). None of these acronyms are problematic if you're a doctor, but they are if you don't know what the acronyms mean.

Jargon is not evil. However, it can be used for evil. It can bamboozle instead of inform, it can exclude people rather than include them and it can make perfectly good pieces of writing completely impenetrable to anyone other than the author. It can also be used in an attempt to disguise the fact that somebody hasn't got a clue what they're on about.

As George Orwell stated (1946), we should never use 'a foreign phrase, a scientific word or a jargon word if you can think of an everyday English equivalent'. There are exceptions, of course: if you're talking SaaS with someone in the IT industry, then jargon's fine. But a great deal of business writing is about communicating with people in different jobs, in different departments or with different areas of expertise, and jargon can get in the way of that.

There's another kind of jargon to beware of. If you've ever played Business Bullshit Bingo in a dull meeting, you'll know exactly what we're talking about.

BAD BUZZ

Buzzwords are jargon that has become fashionable, and they're often incredibly annoying. My pet hate is currently 'surfaced', to mean 'found' or 'showed', but there are plenty more. Get your bingo card ready and see how many of the following you can tick off in meetings:

- mindshare
- empowerment
- leverage
- synergy
- unpack
- sea change
- reach out
- push the envelope
- holistic approach
- new normal
- going forward
- bandwidth
- eating your own dogfood
- pain point
- hyperlocal
- low hanging fruit
- value-added

I could go on for days.

There are two big problems with buzzwords. The first is that there are usually better, simpler words you can use instead, as the example of 'surfaced' demonstrates. But the bigger problem is that when everybody's using them, they become clichéd and meaningless.

Let's look at a few examples from the world of IT.

Best in class

Who decided the firm was the best, and who defined the class they're best in?

Customer-focused

With very few exceptions – we're thinking of a certain budget airline – every organisation with paying customers is customer-focused. If they aren't, they won't stay in business very long.

Exceed expectations

Exceeding expectations is the new 'giving it 110 per cent'. If you've told someone you're going to exceed their expectations, they'll adjust their expectations accordingly, so the best you can do is meet their newly raised expectations.

Value-added solution provider

Every product or service is a solution to a problem or requirement, so that bit's meaningless. And value-added is nonsense, because it implies you're getting something for nothing. You're not, as the supplier's invoices will make abundantly clear.

Turnkey solution to deliver improved ROI

ROI – return on investment – is a key part of any investment: nobody buys a product that's guaranteed to waste all their money. And turnkey solutions – services that you just have to turn a key or press a button to deploy – tend only to exist in marketers' minds.

Imagineering, thought leadership, establishing new paradigms

If anybody uses any of these in a meeting it's okay to hurl them through the nearest window.

WHY YOU SHOULD BANISH BUZZWORDS AND JUNK THE JARGON

There are several very good reasons to avoid buzzwords and jargon.

They're a hindrance, not a help

If you don't know the terms used, they're a barrier to clear communication: nobody has the faintest idea what a manual geomorphological modification implement might be, but we all know what a spade is.

They can undo all your hard work

We often receive press releases and emails so packed with buzzwords and jargon that we genuinely can't work out what they're about. So we delete them, or throw them in the recycling.

They're impersonal

If you Google 'value-added solution provider' you will get more than 73 million results. It's like the climactic scene in *Spartacus* where everybody yells 'I'm *Spartacus*' so that the Roman general can't find the man he wants. That's a great idea if you're trying to stop Roman centurions from stabbing somebody, but in business 'we are exactly the same as everybody else' is a terrible sales pitch.

They raise red flags

To a reader, a buzzword-packed message doesn't necessarily say 'here's a message from someone who really knows their stuff'. It's as likely to say 'here's a load of empty marketing nonsense' or 'here's some more fashionable gibberish from management'. Neither option wins hearts and minds.

They waste words

Like clichés, buzzwords should be used sparingly or avoided altogether. There are usually better, shorter alternatives.

KEY TAKEAWAYS

- Jargon can make writing much harder to read and to understand.

- Avoid obscure words or jargon.

- Buzzwords are often bullshit.

7 MAKE YOUR CASE

All business writing exists to do a particular job. Some jobs are bigger than others. In this chapter you will discover how to make a case for a large investment or other big change to your business.

So far, we've discussed business writing in a general sense, with tips and tricks that are relevant to all kinds of business writing from emails to product pitches. In this chapter we're going to focus on one particular kind of business writing, which is making a case for something. That something might be a proposal to invest in new hardware or software, or it might be a document suggesting better ways to deliver a product or service. It might be for internal company use, or it might be a detailed proposal for a prospective client. In addition to the things we have already covered about successful business writing, there are a few tools and tips that can help you make the strongest case possible and present it in the best possible way.

In some ways, making a case is one of the most straightforward types of business writing you can do. You already know what you want to achieve: you want the person who reads your proposal to do what you suggest or buy what you recommend. All you need to do is persuade them.

HOW TO WIN FRIENDS AND INFLUENCE PEOPLE

Making a compelling case starts just like any other piece of business writing, albeit with a head start because we know what we want to achieve. We then need to identify who our audience is and what they care about.

In many cases, your audience will be your manager or other executives, either inside your own organisation or in a client's or potential client's organisation, and what they care about will be money: saving it, making more of it or wasting less of it. If you can make a persuasive case that doing X will either save or make money – even if it's in abstract terms such as improved morale, better customer satisfaction or better use of resources – then you're likely to receive a sympathetic response.

The best bit of business case writing advice I have seen comes from Carolyn O'Hara, who wrote in the *Harvard Business Review*: 'Lead with the need' (O'Hara, 2014) You've identified something that needs to be changed: here's why it needs to be changed, and here's what you think we should do about it.

If what you're suggesting isn't an enormous or enormously expensive project, then making your case is straightforward. A business case is typically presented in four sections:

i. Explain the problem: lead with the need.
ii. Describe the possible options, including doing nothing.
iii. Recommend the best solution.
iv. Explain how it will be implemented.

If it's going to be a fairly long document, then it's a good idea to start with an executive summary. This is the business equivalent of the film industry's elevator pitch, where you sell a movie idea in a sentence or two – so, for example, *Alien* was '*Jaws* in space', and you could describe the *Twilight* movies as 'Jane Austen meets Dracula'.

It doesn't have to be quite that short – a written executive summary can be many paragraphs long if necessary – but it needs to sell your idea. Leave the detail to the rest of the document. What your executive summary needs to do is make the reader want to know more. Once again, we are using business writing to tell a story, and if you can't sum it up simply, then you're going to find it difficult to enthuse others.

In some cases, your audience might include people with different concerns. The finance director may be concerned about cost control, or the head of HR may worry about how much training and support will be required. If you can anticipate these concerns and answer them in your business case, you'll get a much better reception.

Throughout your business case it's important to be as careful with words as you would be if you were writing an advertisement or brochure. Avoid waffle, jargon and wild guesses, keep your sentences simple and short, and don't present anybody with dense blocks of text. You might not be selling a product, but you are still selling something.

WRITING PRESENTATIONS

I have previously poured scorn on PowerPoint presentations, but they can be very effective if used wisely and they're often very useful when it comes to making a case. As with infographics, less is more: your slides should accompany what you're saying, but they shouldn't simply say what you're saying. If they do, faster readers will speed-read them and ignore you altogether. A single chart with an exciting figure and short caption will have more impact than 10 lines of cramped text.

The first trick to successful presentations is to follow the rule of three, first set out by Aristotle:

     i.   Tell them what you're going to tell them.
    ii.   Tell them.
   iii.   Tell them what you've told them.

Step 1 is your very brief introduction: 'Today I'm going to demonstrate that X will make everybody's life better.' Step 2 is where you make your case. Step 3 is a brief recap of your key point or points: 'As we've discovered, X would make everybody's life better. Is there anything you'd like to ask me?'

Step 2 follows exactly the same structure as making a case in writing. Once again, we tell a story. First of all, we lead with the need – 'here's an issue that needs to be addressed' – and then set out the available options, including doing nothing. From there, we explain why our recommended course of action is the best option, and we then describe how that course of action would be implemented.

Step 3 is the takeaway – and that's something used throughout this book, because it's very effective. It's a quick reminder of the key points you want your reader to focus on.

THREE IS THE MAGIC NUMBER

There's another rule of three in presentations, which is to stick to three main points. That's because our brains like to remember three things at once, and it's why three-point phrases are so common in advertising, speeches and the arts.

For example:

Stop, Look and Listen. (road safety advert)

Our priorities are education, education, education. (Tony Blair speech)

A Mars a day helps you work, rest and play. (advertising slogan for Mars bars)

Friends, Romans, Countrymen, lend me your ears. (Shakespeare's *Julius Caesar*)

Truth, justice and the American way. (what Superman fights for, DC Comics)

Everything feels utterly smooth, fast, and immersive. (Apple iPad Pro website)

Many successful presentations have three sections, share three ideas and have no more than three bullet points on screen at once. It's a trick that also works in many other kinds of business writing too.

IT'S A SHAME ABOUT ROI

Let's say you're an IT manager and you want the board to approve a significant IT investment. What is very important to you – the problems the investment will solve and the opportunities it will create – might not be very important to the board unless you can demonstrate the business benefits. More often than not, that means speaking the language of money – and in particular, return on investment, or ROI for short. If you can demonstrate an acceptable ROI, you are much more likely to get the investment you need.

ROI can be a very simple calculation. First of all, you estimate how much the proposed change will cost. Then, you estimate the financial benefit it will bring. Deduct the cost from the benefit and you've got your ROI, so if an investment of £8,000 would reduce operating costs by £10,000, you have an ROI of £2,000, or 25 per cent. The percentage is calculated against the cost of the investment, in this case £8,000.

Some benefits are easier to quantify than others. For example, your proposed investment might boost the morale of every user in the organisation, but that's hard to put on a spreadsheet. By all means, mention such benefits, but don't try and pin a financial value on them if you're just guessing.

You'll also need to pick a time period. ROI is calculated over a time period, usually the life of a project, because to begin with there are lots of costs and few benefits. By the end of the project that should be reversed: the money's been spent, and the benefits are everywhere. In IT, ROI is usually calculated over three to five years.

Whatever you do, don't rely on guesswork. Prediction is an art rather than a science, but if you're asking the board for money, then you need to put forward a convincing case with realistic numbers. For example, your proposal may be designed to reduce business travel by 10 per cent, or to reduce energy use by 3 per cent, or to free up X hours per person.

HOW TO PRESENT YOUR BUSINESS CASE FOR A LARGE PROJECT

To write a business case for a large project, I would recommend breaking it into four key sections. They are:

- executive summary;
- finance;
- project definition;
- project organisation.

The executive summary is the bird's eye view of the proposal and it's best to write it last, when you have all the facts and figures at your disposal. It's a short summary of the entire business case, and it should tell the person or people reading it everything they need to know without going into detail.

As you would expect, the finance section answers the million-dollar question: how much is this going to cost? This is where you'd break down details such as hardware costs, training costs, support costs, software licences and any other quantifiable expenses. This section should generally include a contingency fund, because projects rarely run entirely to time or budget.

The project definition is where you provide the background to your proposal: here is the issue, here is what I propose to do about it, here are the benefits it will bring and here are the risks, potential limitations and issues it will raise. This is where you'll detail the ROI calculations. In some cases, it's also where you'll show additional financial calculations. More of that in a moment.

Last, but not least, there's the project organisation section, which says who will be doing what and how progress and success will be monitored. Monitoring might involve hard information, such as hours worked or money spent, but you can also standardise monitoring of softer outcomes, such as customer satisfaction, by creating a standard measurement tool such as an online questionnaire.

ROI: PLAN FOR THE BEST BUT TRY TO PREDICT THE WORST

If you're not making a case for expensive long-term investments, you can skip this bit.

Investments don't happen in isolation. Changes in the outside world can make them more expensive or riskier, and your proposal may need to reflect that.

As I write this chapter, the Bank of England has approved the first base rate rise since 2007, raising the cost of borrowing. The cost of electricity has increased by 7.3 per cent since last year, and while diesel is currently around £1.20 per litre, instability in the Middle East means that prices could soar to the same kind of levels we last saw in 2013, when a litre was £1.47. The pound is currently worth $1.31.

All of these changes have an effect. For example, the weak pound means many US IT companies are currently operating dollar-for-pound pricing, so a $999 iPhone X costs £999 here and US-based services that charge in dollars per user per month are more expensive than they were just a few months ago. Components and consumables priced in dollars are more expensive for UK firms than they used to be. Increasing energy prices and fuel prices increases businesses' operating costs.

You don't need to consider these things if you're only asking for a couple of new PCs, but you do if you're proposing a significant long-term investment, because they can affect your ROI. An increase in borrowing costs and operating costs could make your project more expensive to implement, or the benefits less significant. As a result, for large project proposals, it's important to state any underlying assumptions, such as assuming energy prices increase at the same rate or that wage levels won't increase significantly.

For large-scale projects, a tool called the project discount rate is used. It's a kind of reverse interest rate that tells you how much a sum of money you have today will be worth in the future.

Let's say you have £1,000 in your hand today. The interest rate on savings accounts is effectively zero, but the cost of living goes up every year, so the spending power goes down. If the difference is 5 per cent, then £1,000 in today's money will only be worth £950 this time next year. If you've been too optimistic and the difference is 10 per cent, then it will only be worth £900.

When you include that percentage in your cash flow calculations, it's called the project discount rate. If you're confident that your predictive abilities are much better than any astrologer and that the risks to your project are very small, you would use a very low project discount rate. If there's a lot of supposition and risk taking, you would use a high project discount rate.

Let's look at a real example. You're making the case for an IT investment that will cost £10,000, and you expect to generate positive cash flow of an extra £2,500 per year for five years. That's a £2,500 overall benefit, or 25 per cent, in theory at least.

The next step is to use the project discount rate to see what your real ROI is likely to be. The rule of thumb is that the closer to double figures the project discount rate becomes, the more likely the project will deliver a disappointing or even negative ROI.

We'll consider two scenarios here. First, we'll be confident in our predictive powers and go for a low rate of 5 per cent, and then we'll look at the same proposal but with a lot less confidence and a project discount rate of 10 per cent.

To use the project discount rate, you simply apply it to the cash flow prediction for each year – so to take 5 per cent off, you divide it by 1.05. Therefore, after a year, £2,500 in today's money will be £2,309. In year two it will be £2,267; in year three it will be £2,195; in year four it will be £2,056; and in year five it will be £1,958.

In total, then, our £10,000 investment will bring in £10,785. That isn't quite the 25 per cent return we had hoped for, but, at just under 8 per cent, it might be enough to convince the board to go ahead.

What happens when we are less confident in the future? With a rate of 10 per cent instead of 5 per cent, the figures are: £2,272; £2,066; £1,878; £1,707; and £1,523. The total is therefore £9,446, which is a loss of just over 5 per cent. The board might still think the investment is worth it, but it will be a much tougher sell.

Clearly, we are looking at worst case scenarios here, but that's an important part of making your case. If you don't consider the worst case scenario, the board surely will.

KEY TAKEAWAYS

- Always lead with the need.
- Don't rely on guesswork and always check your figures.
- Remember the rule of threes.

8 WRITING FOR ROBOTS: BUSINESS WRITING FOR THE INTERNET

In this chapter you will learn the difference between writing for print and writing for websites, and why you should never promise a three-legged man if you don't have one.

There are three kinds of writing for the internet. There's the writing you do for Google; the writing you do in an email; and the writing you do for social media. They have a lot in common, but there are some crucial differences too.

WRITING FOR GOOGLE

Let's start with Google.

In the early days of internet search engines, search results were based on the words a page contained. That was perfectly sensible, because if you were looking for a book such as *Fly Fishing* by J.R. Hartley (1991), then a page containing the words 'fly fishing' and 'JR Hartley' was likely to be relevant. The more times the words appeared, the more relevant the page was likely to be.

Unfortunately, a lot of people soon realised that they could game the system. By stuffing their pages with popular but irrelevant keywords, they could make their sites appear in search results for those keywords.

It wasn't quite as bad as this:

> If Britney Spears had a driveway she'd buy her gravel from Gravel Direct, your one stop shop for all things gravel. Our gravel's so good that when you've ordered from us once, you'll soon be back saying Hit Me Baby One More Time, just like Britney Spears. And our gravel isn't Toxic, like Britney Spears' new single.

but it was still pretty bad.

Another tactic was to use relevant keywords, but to overuse them. Here is an example that Google uses to illustrate the problem:[6]

> We sell custom cigar humidors. Our custom cigar humidors are handmade. If you're thinking of buying a custom cigar humidor, please contact our custom cigar humidor specialists at *custom.cigar.humidors@example.com*.

If you've ever searched for products online, you'll also be familiar with pages that do this:

> Are you looking for Black Friday deals? If you're looking for the best Black Friday deals you'll find the best Black Friday deals right here. We look for the best Black Friday deals and put them on our best Black Friday deals page where you can find the best Black Friday deals on Black Friday. We find the best Black Friday deals on laptops and the best Black Friday deals on monitors, as well as the best Black Friday deals on accessories.

Don't do that. Not only is it horrible to read – and likely to provoke fury if, after wading through it, the page doesn't actually have the thing your reader is looking for – but Google now penalises any website that uses such tricks.

Google visibility matters, particularly in Europe where it has nearly 100 per cent market share for search. If Google doesn't like your writing, searchers won't see it. That won't matter

---

[6] See https://support.google.com/webmasters/answer/66358?hl=en

if you're writing online content for people who already know who you are and who will seek out such content, but if you want to reach a wider audience you need to appease the Google gods.

Here's how to do it.

SEO: HOW TO DO IT THE RIGHT WAY

Search engine optimisation (SEO) is the process of writing in such a way that your page or pages turn up when people search for that particular topic, issue or product. It's also a moving target, because whenever Google tightens up the rules to stop people gaming the system, people find new ways to game the system. The latest version of Google's SEO documentation is online at www.google.com/webmasters/docs/search-engine-optimization-starter-guide.pdf.

The specifics of SEO may change, but the basics don't. If you want to rank highly in search engine results, you need to deliver what people are searching for without wasting their time.

Think of your own searches. What annoys you when you're trying to find information or solve a problem? My list includes:

- irrelevant content;
- unreliable content;
- false promises, such as products or answers the site doesn't actually have;
- writing that goes on and on and on and on and on and on and on and ...

Search engines attempt to prioritise sites on the basis of accuracy, relevancy and trustworthiness. If your content meets all three criteria, it will naturally score highly in search results.

There are some technical considerations too. There are things Google prefers to see in the HTML code of web pages, such as accurate title tags, descriptive page addresses and short page summaries, but the most important bit of Google advice is much more straightforward:

> Users know good content when they see it and will likely want to direct other users to it. This could be through blog posts, social media services, email, forums, or other means. Organic or word-of-mouth buzz is what helps build your site's reputation with both users and Google, and it rarely comes without quality content.

As with other forms of business writing, your writing should be designed to do something. When you're writing for an external audience that's coming via search, you need to offer something useful. Most of the time, when people are searching they're usually trying to solve a problem – a practical problem, or a lack of knowledge about something. For example, my most recent searches have been to look for refurbished laptops, to see if other people are having the same broadband issues as me and to work out how to change the clock in the car. If your writing isn't designed to solve a problem, it might not need to be written in the first place.

The basic rules of writing apply just as much online, so brevity, simplicity and accuracy are essential. But there are some other online-only considerations. The most important one is that you should not try to trick your readers into visiting pages that are not relevant by making promises you can't keep.

Another important tip is when you're linking to something else: don't just say 'click here'. That's useless to people using assistive technology such as screen reader software. If you're linking to a report or a support document, say what it is in the link text. For similar reasons, don't use images containing text when you could just use text.

TL;DR

There's a famous acronym on the internet: tl;dr. It's short for 'too long; didn't read', and it sums up the way people read on the internet. If it doesn't grab them quickly, they will move on to something else.

In a famous study by internet accessibility expert Jakob Nielsen back in 1997, researchers discovered that people don't read web pages. They scan them, casting their eyes over them at high speed. When Nielsen's team studied internet users, they found that 79 per cent always scanned web pages and just 16 per cent read word by word (Nielsen, 1997).

Nielsen's research was carried out on desktop PC users. In 2016, the study was repeated for mobile devices. The key takeaway is that it's harder to read on a phone than a PC. It slows down reading and reduces users' ability to comprehend what they're reading. In effect, a smartphone makes us less smart (Meyer, 2016).

If you're writing for mobile, that means it's important to simplify wherever you can. And whether you're writing for mobile or desktop users, Nielsen's advice is just as relevant today as it was in 1997. Always use:

- one idea per paragraph;
- half the word count you would use for print;
- meaningful sub-headings, not clever or jokey ones;
- bulleted lists, like this one;
- plain language, not marketing speak.

These recommendations were tested for usability, which is based on multiple measurements including:

- how long it took readers to find specific information in the content;
- how many readers did not find the right information;

- how well readers remembered the key points;
- how satisfied readers were with the content.

Halving the word count increased usability by 58 per cent. Presenting numbers as bulleted lists rather than a paragraph of text improved usability by 47 per cent. Using neutral rather than exaggerated, overhyped language improved usability by 27 per cent. And using all three techniques improved usability by 124 per cent.

WHAT TO DO ABOUT LONG DOCUMENTS

Some documents can't be shortened without making them useless: a detailed proposal, an important case study, a procedures manual or an in-depth guide to a product simply don't lend themselves to a handful of sentences. That leaves you with two choices: you can either provide the information as an embedded document, or you can break it up into shorter, more readable sections – either in newspaper-style formatting with sections divided up by sub-headings and images or other media, or into multiple separate pages.

Embedding is the easiest option: it's just a matter of uploading the PDF or Word document to your site or a sharing service such as Dropbox and providing a link to it. It's an approach best suited to lengthy documents for people using desktop PCs, laptops or tablets: PDFs in particular are a pain to read on smartphones.

As with writing for the internet, avoid unnecessary design clutter and focus on readability. Just because you don't have to optimise it for the internet, doesn't mean it shouldn't be optimised at all.

WRITING FOR EMAIL NEWSLETTERS

Many businesses like to send out email newsletters, and we've got some bad news about that: in the studies mentioned earlier in this chapter, Nielsen's researchers found that people are even less patient with email than they are online.

That doesn't mean that email doesn't work. It does, and it's a crucial marketing tool for many businesses – many of whom use dedicated email platforms such as MailChimp or Constant Contact to help them manage and monitor their campaigns – but emails need to be well designed, precision targeted and well written.

The most important thing to remember is that we are all absolutely drowning in email, and it's getting worse. The average office worker receives 121 emails a day, and 47 per cent of those are spam.[7]

Email is increasingly mobile, too. In 2017, 66 per cent of email was read on mobile devices. On PCs and Macs, the click-through rate for marketing emails – that is, the percentage of people who click on the action link after reading the message – is 18 per cent. On mobile that falls to 13.7 per cent. Your email is more likely to be read if you send it on a Tuesday, and the ideal subject line is between 60 and 70 characters long.

As with writing for web pages and blogs, writing for email is all about getting your message across as quickly as possible. You have a very short window before the reader's attention moves elsewhere, so you must fight the flab even more than you do in other forms of business writing.

There are a few useful things to consider with writing for emails:

- They should work without images. Images take much longer to load than text, and on spotty mobile connections they sometimes don't load at all.

- If you have a call to action, such as a 'Click Here For More!' button, it should be near the top so that readers can click on it without having to scroll to find it.

---

[7] See www.radicati.com/wp/wp-content/uploads/2017/01/Email-Statistics-Report-2017-2021-Executive-Summary.pdf

- And, of course, your subject line should make readers want to click on it to find out more.

The golden rule of writing for email is simple:

Don't annoy your readers.

Email newsletters are not just a sales channel, and overly sales-y content will have the recipients reaching for the unsubscribe link.

A newsletter must provide value. That value could be in the form of useful industry insights, news of important technological breakthroughs, how-to advice, tips, industry-specific humour or photos of cats sitting on servers. Anything that's useful or interesting to your readers, relevant to what they do and relevant to what your business does.

Once you have identified the content of your newsletter, the next step is to work on the pitch: how are you going to sell the idea of your newsletter so that your clients or potential clients happily click on the 'Subscribe' button?

There are two key sections to that. First of all, you need a good headline and strapline to urge the reader to subscribe. For example:

Get Cats on Servers – free every Friday!
You love cats. You love servers. Get cats on servers, fresh every Friday.

Second, you need to sell the content of your newsletter. Keep it short and punchy, for example:

A weekly email of the very funniest photos of cats on servers.

No dogs. No desktops. Just felines at home and the odd Cat6 cable.

Obviously, this proposed content is here for comedic effect, but we've made it abundantly clear what our newsletter contains and when it's published. Your newsletter might be about industry news, or top tips for particular products, but remember to sell the *sizzle*, not the sausage.

SOMEONE INVENTED A NEW WAY TO GET READERS; YOU'LL NEVER GUESS WHAT HAPPENS NEXT!

One of the worst developments on the internet is the rise of clickbait, which is when an email, Twitter post, Facebook message or website headline promises some kind of astonishing information but won't tell you what it is until you click through to see the article. That way, the website gets all-important page views and advertising views before the reader even knows what's in the article.

The reason it's so popular is because it works.

Clickbait takes advantage of something called a 'curiosity gap', which dates back to the days of movie matinees. In the golden days of cinema serials, cowboy films or other thrilling things would end with a cliffhanger – often literally, with the hero hanging off a cliff with no obvious means of escape. How could he possibly survive? Find out in the next episode!

The curiosity gap is why TV presenters say 'find out after the break' and why every single internet headline appears to follow the 'Click here to discover the one simple trick that'll make your business better' template.

There's nothing wrong with clickbait if you deliver what you promise. It's when you don't that readers get annoyed. As James Hamblin put it beautifully in an article for *The Atlantic* magazine (Hamblin, 2014), if you're going to use a headline such as 'This Three-Legged Man Is Not What You're Thinking But Will Blow Your Mind. You Won't Believe How Three-Legged He Is Until You Click. It's a Real Third Leg, Not a Crutch, I Promise', you had better deliver.

If you promise me a three-legged man, and I go into your Internet tent and there is a real three-legged man, then, fair enough. I have more questions and feel pity for this man and hope he's fully on board with being paraded about like this, but apart from that, okay. If instead you reveal to me a man with a crutch, then I definitely hate you and feel no sympathy for your crutch-ed accomplice, even though he's clearly injured. That kind of deception is obviously one way to get readers to call your article clickbait. Even if what you wrote is great, people will be upset if it under-delivers on the expectations set by the headline. If you promise me a three-legged man and I go into the tent and it's a sword swallower, I'm upset, even if he's really terrifyingly amazing and highly regarded in sword-swallowing circles.

Unfortunately, an awful lot of internet headlines promise a three-legged man and deliver a two-legged man with a crutch. It's terribly short-term and self-defeating: you might get extra readers with such trickery, but those readers are not going to share your content or fall for it the next time you do it.

It's all about keeping your promises. If you promise three tips that will truly transform a business, those tips had better be good ones the reader won't already know. And if they are, that's great. Your reader will be happy and may well share your message with other like-minded souls. But, like anything else in business, if you over-promise and under-deliver, you're going to annoy people.

So how do you write a good headline? A headline should quickly answer three key questions:

- What is this?
- Why does it matter?
- Why should I read it?

A good headline does that in the most effective possible way.

Depending on who you're writing for and what you're writing about, you can use a variety of tricks to make your headlines work harder. For example:

- **Use numbers:** '73% faster X'; '39% better Y'; '6 mistakes your rivals are making'.

- **Use odd numbers:** we see these as more trustworthy. A list of 11 things suggests it wouldn't fit into a 10-thing template; a list of 10 was probably padded out to have a nice even number.

- **Don't use words if you can use digits:** '7' is more effective and uses fewer characters than 'seven'.

- **Have a clear reason for reading:** what's in the piece?

- **Don't use 'things':** there's always a better, more interesting word such as 'tips', 'facts', 'secrets' or 'strategies'.

- **Be specific:** in business, very specific headlines work very well. '5 proven ways to slash your IT support overhead' is more interesting than '5 ways to cut costs'.

- **Be urgent:** A good headline makes the reader want the information *now*.

KEY TAKEAWAYS

- Don't try to fool Google.

- On the internet, people scan text rather than read it.

- Don't over-promise and under-deliver.

9   BE YOUR OWN AUDIENCE

It's time to talk about editing. In this chapter you will discover why it's even more important than writing. It's the process of taking what you've written and making it as good as it can possibly be.

No matter how much effort and expertise you've put into your writing, the first version can almost always be improved. There's a reason newspapers, magazines and book publishers employ editors: they take the writers' work and make it better.

Some types of business writing will require other people to read and criticise your work. For example, you might be writing about something that the firm's lawyers need to approve. Or you might be writing something that will go up on the company blog and the marketing people want to make sure you communicate a particular message. But even if you don't have to do those things, your writing will still benefit from editing.

If you have a colleague who can cast a critical eye over your writing and make constructive suggestions, that's great. If you don't, you can be your own editor.

But first ...

LET GO OF YOUR EGO

When you're editing a piece of writing, you've got to take a step back. Yes, you should be proud of it. And yes, you deserve to be carried around the office on your colleagues' shoulders for producing such a great piece of work. But that doesn't mean you can't make it even better.

It's really important that you're open to criticism, especially from other people. Writers love to moan about editors being their 'natural enemy', as *Game of Thrones* author George R.R. Martin puts it with his tongue firmly in his cheek (Martin, 1979), but very few people don't benefit from editors or editing. It's like optimising code, removing duplicate data or compressing files. You've created something, and now you want to maximise its efficiency.

There are four key things to look for when you're editing:

    i.   simplicity;
    ii.   brevity;
    iii. accuracy;
    iv. effectiveness.

Let's take each one in turn.

SIMPLICITY

Appropriately enough, this one's simple. You're looking for anything that makes your writing less friendly to the reader: too-long paragraphs, unnecessary use of big words, the passive voice, jargon and anything else that might make the reader go 'eh?'.

BREVITY

If your memo about the office fridge is six pages long, it probably needs to be cut down a bit. It's very easy to write too much – we do it all the time because it's often easier to write too much and then make it punchy by cutting it down – and some of the things mentioned in Chapter 5, 'Fight The Flab', are easy to spot and take out. For example, the passive voice ('it was decided that') and irrelevant background information should be the first things to go.

When you're editing a piece of business writing, the constant question should be: does it need this? Would this paragraph work just as well without that sentence, or that sentence work just as well without those words? If the answer is yes, cut out the bits you don't need.

ACCURACY

Accuracy is particularly important if you're communicating detailed instructions for somebody to follow, or if you're describing something compulsory, such as regulations on data protection, or if you're using figures. However, it also applies to every kind of business writing. Are you presenting your personal opinion as a fact? You should make that clear (assuming, of course, that the piece of writing wouldn't benefit from cutting that bit out completely). Are any sections unclear? Pretend you don't know all the things you know about the subject. Is there anything that would make you scratch your head in confusion?

Don't forget about spelling, grammar and punctuation too. Automatic spellcheckers and grammar checkers are reasonably good, but they don't always catch things such as homophones, which are words that sound the same but are spelled differently. 'Their', 'they're' and 'there' are homophones. So are write/right, to/two and mail/male. If you are relying on a computer's spelling or grammar checker it's a good idea to get a colleague to look over your work as well.

Last, but not least, watch out for excessive capitalisation: using caps LIKE THIS is perceived as shouting, and blocks of capitalised text are tiring to read.

EFFECTIVENESS

Remember when I said you should never start writing until you know what you're trying to achieve? It's time to see if you've done what you set out to do. Does the writing make it clear what, if anything, you want the reader to do? Have you stuck to the topic without going off on tangents or cramming some unrelated things into the same document? Have you got your point across as effectively as possible? Are you using positive action words that make things sound interesting?

One of the best ways to check for all of these things is to read your writing out loud. Sentences that look just fine on paper can have you gasping for breath long before you reach the end. Clichés tend to sound trite when you say them aloud. And the very fact you feel a bit daft speaking out loud means you'll have a lot less tolerance for overly wordy or woolly language.

Another way to spot bits you can improve is to print your writing onto paper, take a bit of time away from it and then look at the printout with fresh eyes. There's something about reading on screens that makes it easy to miss mistakes; when you read the same thing from paper, the mistakes jump out at you.

For some kinds of business writing, the best way to measure its effectiveness is to get other people to try it out. For example, if you are writing a guide to a new software package or setting out a new procedure, getting others to test it out and provide feedback can be invaluable. It's a particularly good way to spot the kind of assumptions we all make when we know a subject inside out: what's really obvious to us might not be obvious to somebody else, and their feedback enables us to fill in any gaps that might cause confusion.

Think of it like driving a car. So many of the things you do when driving are completely automatic. You don't need to remember which pedal to press when you want to brake, or what you need to do to change gear, or where the windscreen wipers are. But when you sat in a car for the first time, you didn't know any of those things. The same applies to someone who has just joined the department, or who hasn't encountered a particular system or policy before. Testing and getting feedback helps you to identify any bits that need to go into a little bit more detail.

KEY TAKEAWAYS

- Everyone benefits from editing.
- Test and get feedback from others where you can.
- Always ask: does the document really need this bit?

10 COMMUNICATING GOODWILL AND DELIVERING BAD NEWS

So far, we've focused on very business-y business writing: proposals, marketing, guidelines, procedures and other common kinds of business documents. But there's another kind of business writing: communicating goodwill and delivering bad news.

In this chapter you will learn the most effective ways to deliver even the most awful news, and how to let people down gently without hurting their feelings.

GOODWILL HUNTING

By goodwill we don't mean the financial value of a business's customers. We mean positive, co-operative, friendly feelings. That might be the feelings of the people you work with, or the feelings of clients or other important external people. It's not something you can put a financial value on, but happy staff and happy customers do tend to mean a healthier balance sheet.

You don't need to put goodwill messages in writing – sometimes an instant message, tweet or phone call is perfectly appropriate – but there's something about a formal email or handwritten note that amplifies the feel-good factor.

The most effective goodwill messages follow these simple rules:

- **Be timely:** send your message when the reason for sending it is still current. A warm welcome to a new member of staff doesn't seem so warm if the new hire has been in post for a month.

- **Be direct:** get to the point immediately, whether you're thanking someone for their efforts or offering sympathy for their loss.

- **Be specific:** if you're praising someone, highlight a particular thing they did.

- **Be sincere:** don't over-egg the pudding, use language you wouldn't normally use or fall back on buzzwords.

- **Be short:** make your point, don't labour it.

For example:

Jane —

I just wanted to thank you for all your efforts on the Megacorp plans. I know you put in a lot of hours on this one, and it's really paid off. Jim called me earlier to say it's one of the most compelling proposals he's ever read, and when you think how many pitches he's seen over the years, that's high praise indeed. I really appreciate all the work you've done on this one.

Or:

Bill —

Thanks again for your time earlier. I'm really excited about the new project and so glad to be part of it.

Or:

Nadia —

I just saw the news of your promotion. Congratulations! It's about time they recognised your genius. Let's meet up for coffee soon and you can tell me all about it. So happy for you!

I don't normally recommend exclamation marks in business writing, but of course they're fine for informal, friendly communications. Just try not to use too many! They get annoying!!!

For more formal relationships, such as those with clients, stick to more formal language such as:

> Tom,
>
> Congratulations on winning the Innovator award. It's well deserved – it's such a great product, and I'm really glad to see the team getting the credit they're due for all that hard work. I'm sure this is the first of many such awards.

It doesn't take much time to send a goodwill note, but the positive effects last a long time. Even in business, it's nice to be nice.

NOW FOR THE BAD NEWS

Sometimes we need to communicate bad news. That might be to reject a proposal, or to announce changes that won't make people happy. It might be a complaint you're making, or a response to a complaint about someone in the company. Let's look at some examples.

Saying no to someone's big idea

One of your colleagues has had a brilliant idea for doing things differently. Unfortunately, it would cost much more than it would save, or it would cause more problems than it would solve, or it might not be viable at the moment. Blunt honesty might be the most truthful way to reply, but, as Mary Poppins famously put it, 'a spoonful of sugar helps the medicine go down'.[8]

The best way to say no is to do so in a positive way. That sounds odd, I know, but the following approach really does work:

---

[8] From the Walt Disney film *Mary Poppins* (1964).

- Thank the person for taking the time and effort to put forward their idea.

- Find some positives to praise in their suggestion.

- Explain that, unfortunately, it's a non-starter because...

- Thank and praise them again.

For example:

> Dave —
>
> Thanks so much for your memo. I really appreciate you taking the time and effort to come up with such an interesting and well-argued proposal.
>
> I agree that hardware is an ongoing problem for us and I particularly liked your suggestion about migrating as much as we can to the cloud. Unfortunately, though, our arrangement with ACME means we are locked in for another year at least, so we can't really make any big changes to our core systems for the next 12 months. But you're right, it's something we should really think about when it's time to review our supplier arrangements. I'll keep this handy for when we do that.
>
> Thanks again for all your efforts and please keep the good ideas coming. We're so lucky to have you on the team!
>
> Regards,
>
> Sue

The objective here is to say no in a way that doesn't hurt the person's feelings or discourage them from making more suggestions in the future.

Making a complaint

We have all seen the hilarious (and often fake) complaint letters on the internet featuring heavy sarcasm, liberal use of expletives and the odd purple-faced explosion of fury. So have the people who deal with incoming complaints, so such tactics are ineffective (and if you're representing an organisation, inappropriate and unprofessional).

Complaints are where the golden rule of business writing – know what you're trying to achieve – often goes to die: we'll happily write page after page of forensic detail in barely suppressed fury without actually saying what we want the recipient to do.

As ever, there are some useful questions to ask:

> **Who are you writing to?** *Is it customer service in general, or a specific individual? Will that individual ever receive your communication, or will it just be sent to customer service anyway?*

> **What are you complaining about?** *Is it a specific failure or a pattern of poor service? Is it something the company has total control over?*

> **What evidence do you have?** *Where possible, back up your claims with proof.*

> **What do you want your letter to achieve?** *If you just want to make someone at the company reconsider their life choices, don't write your letter. Are you looking for an apology? Compensation? Seeing the CEO fired out of a giant cannon?*

> **What do you expect the company to do, and when?** *Don't leave the recipient guessing. Make it clear what you want and when you expect a response.*

No matter how angry you are, don't take it out on the reader. In many cases, the person who actually receives your complaint will not have any connection with anything or anyone you're complaining about. In large organisations, they're often overworked and on the receiving end of anger from people they have never communicated with before. Not only is that unfair, but it usually backfires too. Nobody puts in extra effort for people who are not nice to them.

Communicating other kinds of bad news

Some kinds of bad news have to be communicated in very specific ways; for example, anything to do with HR matters – disciplinary letters, redundancy notices, rejecting job applicants and so on – is best left to HR. However, sometimes you may have to communicate news that you know is going to upset people.

We can't take the sting out of bad news, but we can take steps to ensure we don't add insult to injury. Ideally, really bad news should be delivered in person to small groups, but if that isn't possible, then there are some crucial steps to follow when you're delivering bad news in writing.

Take responsibility

We all want to be liked, and of course, being the bearer of bad news tends to affect that. But the recipients won't warm to you if you try to blame others or present yourself as the real victim of the situation.

Be apologetic

No matter how valid the reasons for a course of action, if it's going to have a negative effect on people, you need to acknowledge that in the tone of your letter, email or memo.

Get to the point

Don't beat around the bush. Make it clear what is happening or going to happen.

Use clear language

Euphemisms make the messenger seem dishonest. If something is being cancelled, say cancelled. If it's being shut down, say it's being shut down. If the pay rise isn't going to happen this year, say so.

Accentuate the positive

If there are any positives, mention them – but don't oversell them or try to convince people that everything's fantastic if it isn't.

Explain, but don't over-explain

Communicate the reason for the decision, but don't go into excessive detail. For example, if you're freezing overtime in unexpectedly tough economic conditions because the alternative is to lay off staff, people will understand that. You don't need to provide five paragraphs of justification.

Make the next steps clear

If the news you're sharing will have specific effects on the people you're writing to, make it clear what they are. For example, if a project is cancelled will people be moved to other projects? When? How? By whom? If the recipient wants to talk about this with someone, who do they go to?

Don't personalise it

You may think it's a terrible shame or a necessary evil, but your feelings and opinions are not relevant or appropriate here.

Don't try to lighten the mood

There's a time and a place for humour. This isn't it.

Be empathetic

Put yourself in the place of the people who will be reading your message. How is it going to make them feel? Re-read your writing from that perspective. Is there anything here that might rub salt into the wound or cause unnecessary confusion?

Communicating bad news is never easy or enjoyable, but if you follow the steps above you can make sure it isn't any more unpleasant than it needs to be.

KEY TAKEAWAYS

- Congratulatory messages can improve morale and make clients and colleagues happier.

- Complaints are not for ranting. Make it clear what you want.

- With bad news, don't waffle or try to sugar-coat things.

11 WHAT TO DO WHEN THE WORDS WON'T COME

We've all heard of writer's block, the famous problem where the words won't come when we need them to. And many of us are familiar with the feeling of staring at a blank Word document without the faintest idea of how to start. But the evil powers of writer's block have been vastly overhyped, and it's a problem that you can easily beat.

In this chapter you will learn how to tame writer's block – and why sometimes it's better to go to the gym or have a biscuit.

HAVE A DEADLINE

Writers like to joke and moan about deadlines – the late Douglas Adams famously said that what he loved about deadlines was 'the whooshing noise they make as they go by' (Adams, 2003) – but reasonable deadlines help concentrate the mind. If the deadline for a piece is 'as soon as possible' or 'whenever you can', it's all too easy to forget about it while you focus on more demanding things.

BREAK IT INTO BITS

If it's a big job, take the same approach you would to a big IT project: break it down into smaller pieces and tackle them individually. Big projects often seem intimidating because of their sheer size, but when you look at the individual pieces, suddenly things seem much more achievable.

WRITE AN OUTLINE

It's much easier to put flesh on bones if you actually have some bones to begin with. An outline provides the skeleton of your piece, so, for example, you might work out what key sections you will have and what key bits need to be in each section. Once you've done that, the writing often takes care of itself.

DON'T START AT THE START

If you're having trouble getting started, write a different bit instead: the end, perhaps, or a chunk in the middle. Sometimes it's like jump-starting a car. Once you get moving, the engine kicks in and you are firing on all cylinders.

DON'T STOP

Let's stick with our car analogy a bit longer. You can't just jump-start the car, drive a few yards and then stop again. You need to drive long enough to charge the battery so that you won't end up stuck again. It's exactly the same with writing. Once you've jump-started your writing, keep the momentum going by continuing to write.

FORGET ABOUT PERFECT

Worry about perfection when you're editing. For now, concentrate on getting words down on paper or on the screen. Don't worry if you could put it better or if you haven't quite got the point across as best you can. You can polish it all later.

HAVE A KITKAT®

I'm not being funny – if your blood sugar is a bit low, it can be hard to concentrate. Taking a break for a snack, lunch, a walk or a gym session can often help inspiration strike.

GO AND DO SOMETHING ELSE

Here is something you don't hear in business very much: if at first you don't succeed, give up. If you've tried everything above and the page is still stubbornly blank, go and do something else and come back to it later.

KEY TAKEAWAYS

- Writer's block happens to everyone.
- Don't let perfectionism get in the way.
- Still no luck? Go and do something else.

12 THE BUSINESS WRITING HOUSE OF HORRORS

It's good to end on a positive note, and what could be more positive than pointing out other people's misfortunes? Here are some good examples of when writing goes bad.

This chapter isn't just about enjoying other people's mistakes, although of course that's part of the fun. It's also about how easily some major PR disasters could have been avoided with a little more thinking and a few simple checks.

AVIVA ACCIDENTALLY FIRES ITS ENTIRE WORKFORCE

In 2012, insurance company Aviva dismissed one of its employees, and sent an email asking that person to surrender company property and leave immediately.[9] Unfortunately, HR sent it to all 1,300 employees of its investment division, 1,299 of whom were presumably rather surprised to discover that they were being sacked. A second email eventually clarified things, but the moral of the story is to always check who you're sending your message to.

I often leave the recipient's address to the very last minute so that I don't accidentally send something to the wrong person or send a message before it's ready to be read.

---

[9] See www.bloomberg.com/news/articles/2012-04-20/aviva-fires-everyone-great-moments-in-employee-motivation

ELOP NEEDS SOME HELOP

In 2011 Stephen Elop, appointed CEO of Nokia after its acquisition by Microsoft, sent all employees what is widely regarded to be one of the worst company memos of all time. Dubbed the 'burning platform' memo for his gloomy description of Nokia's market position, the memo began by taking a cheerful approach and rambled on amiably for more than a dozen paragraphs before telling employees that, by the way, all their products were terrible and a whole bunch of people were going to be made redundant. The memo leaked to the press and did serious damage to Nokia's brand and its share price.[10]

Finnish journalists covering Nokia described Elop as one of the worst CEOs in history and said that the memo 'has become a legendary example of how a CEO can destroy everything in just one stroke'. Nokia was worth €29.5 billion when Elop took charge. That fell below €11 billion over the next three years.

PROOF THAT SPELL CHECKING MATTERS

In early 2016, a text message from an English primary school went viral. It was sent to parents to remind them about the Easter church service and added: 'If we can wash your dirty willies, please bring them along. Thank you.'

According to *The Sun*, a clarification was sent six minutes later: 'I am so sorry, it's WELLIES!!! WELLINGTON BOOTS. Sincere apologies for any offence caused.'[11]

WHY DAMORE SHOULD HAVE WRITTEN LESS

In late 2017, a Google engineer called James Damore posted an article to an internal discussion forum about 'Google's

---

[10] See www.theguardian.com/technology/blog/2011/feb/09/nokia-burning-platform-memo-elop

[11] See www.thesun.co.uk/archives/news/1105575/cock-up-as-school-accidentally-sends-out-x-rated-text-message-in-church-announcement/

Ideological Echo Chamber'. In his article he cherry-picked data and misrepresented scientific studies to demonstrate that Google's focus on diversity was bad for the company and that the best employees were young, white men like James Damore.

It leaked, of course, and reached the attention of Google CEO Sundar Pichai, who promptly sacked him. In a memo to all employees, Pichai wrote:[12]

> ... portions of the memo violate our Code of Conduct and cross the line by advancing harmful gender stereotypes in our workplace. Our job is to build great products for users that make a difference in their lives. To suggest a group of our colleagues have traits that make them less biologically suited to that work is offensive and not OK. It is contrary to our basic values and our Code of Conduct, which expects 'each Googler to do their utmost to create a workplace culture that is free of harassment, intimidation, bias and unlawful discrimination'.

WHY JACK GOT ATTACKED

In 2015, Twitter head Jack Dorsey wrote to all his employees: 'Emails like this are usually riddled with corporate speak so I'm going to give it to you straight ...', before immediately launching into corporate speak. A few hundred words later he mentioned that the firm was laying off 8 per cent of its workforce, more than 300 people.[13]

WHEN HASHTAGS GO BAD

The PR team behind Susan Boyle's album launch thought that creating a Twitter hashtag was a good idea. And it was,

---

[12] See www.blog.google/topics/diversity/note-employees-ceo-sundar-pichai/

[13] See www.independent.co.uk/news/business/news/jack-dorsey-twitter-memo-10-of-fice-jargon-phrases-you-should-never-use-a6693456.html

but unfortunately they chose #susanalbumparty. It got lots of attention, but not for the reason the PR team intended...[14]

THE WORST MOTIVATIONAL MEMO EVER

In 2007 Royal Dutch Shell executive David Greer was forced to resign after sending employees a memo voted by readers of the *FT* as the worst motivational memo of all time. It turned out to be plagiarised, with much of it coming from a famous speech by US General George S. Patton, and it began a series of reports questioning Greer's suitability for his job.

It's one of the worst things I have ever read. Highlights – if you can call them that – included:[15]

The introduction:

> Pipeliners All! Many thanks to all of you for your contributions to this week's Bi-Annual Challenge ... and what a Challenge it is going to be for all of us! From the outset, I want to assure you that, despite the mutterings on the day and the challenges ahead, I have total faith in you and our collective ability to complete the task ahead of us.

The darkening mood:

> However, some of the comments and body language witnessed at the Bi-Annual Challenge meeting do suggest that PDP is running the risk of becoming a team that doesn't want to fight and lacks confidence in its own ability. Surely, this is not the case? Pipeliners and Engineers love to fight and win, traditionally. All real engineers love the sting and clash of challenge.

The section where it gets a bit much:

---

[14] See www.nme.com/blogs/hashtags-twitter-10-birthday-susan-boyle-2127822
[15] See www.ft.com/content/80ddc198-139c-11dc-9866-000b5df10621

When everyone of you were kids, I am sure that you all admired the champion marble player, the fastest runner, the toughest boxer, the big league football players. Personally, I, like most others, love winning. I despise cowards and play to win all of the time. This is what I expect of each and everyone of you ... Strive to be proud and confident in yourselves, be proud of your tremendous pipeline achievements to date and lift up your level of personal and team energy to show everyone that you are a winning team capable to achieving this year's goals. If you can crack this angle, I am very confident you can crack the job, with ease.

And, finally, the inspirational ending:

So Lead me, Follow me or Get out of my way; Success is how we bounce when we are on the bottom.

As *The Moscow Times* put it:[16]

In substituting 'pipeliners and engineers' for Patton's 'American he-men' heroes Greer's memo reads more like a cross with a pep talk by David Brent, the haplessly self-deluding boss from the BBC's television comedy show *The Office*.

KEY TAKEAWAYS

- Always ask: what's the worst way this could be interpreted?
- Check your spelling and select Twitter hashtags very carefully.
- Nothing any of us write will be as bad as David Greer's motivational memo.

---

[16] See https://old.themoscowtimes.com/sitemap/free/2007/6/article/sakhalin-pep-talk-from-old-blood-and-guts/196402.html/

AFTERWORD

Business writing has a lot in common with coding or scripting: it can seem pretty frightening to the uninitiated; it can usually benefit from being optimised; and the people who do it for a living sometimes make it seem a lot more difficult than it actually is. But whether it's writing corporate copy or crafting computer code, the process is actually really very simple.

First, you identify the objective that you want to achieve.

Second, you create the words or code necessary to achieve that objective.

Third, you optimise and test what you've created to ensure it does what you want efficiently, effectively and with no alarms and no surprises.

As the poet Matthew Arnold wrote in the late nineteenth century (McPherson Shilling and Fuller, 1997: 225):

> People think that I can teach them style. What stuff it all is! Have something to say, and say it as clearly as you can. That is the only secret of style.

Happy writing.

REFERENCES

Adams, Douglas (2003) *The Salmon of Doubt: Hitchhiking the Galaxy One Last Time*. Ballantine Books, New York.

Bernoff, Josh (2016) 'Bad writing is destroying your company's productivity'. *Harvard Business Review*. Available at: https://hbr.org/2016/09/Bad-Writing-Is-Destroying-Your-Companys-Productivity

Hamblin, James (2014) 'It's everywhere, the clickbait'. *The Atlantic*. Available at: www.theatlantic.com/entertainment/archive/2014/11/clickbait-what-is/382545/

Hartley, J.R. (1991) *Fly Fishing: Memories of Angling Days*. Ishi Press, New York.

Martin, George R.R. (1979) 'Editors: The writer's natural enemy'. The Guest of Honour speech, delivered at Coastcon II, Biloxi, Mississippi, on 10 March 1979. Available at: https://www.georgerrmartin.com/about-george/speeches/editors-the-writers-natural-enemy/

McPherson Shilling, Lilless and Fuller, Linda K. (1997) *Dictionary of Quotations in Communications*. Greenwood Publishing Group, Westport (CT).

Meyer, Kate (2016) 'Reading content on mobile devices'. Nielsen Norman Group, Fremont (CA). Available at: www.nngroup.com/articles/mobile-content/

Nielsen, Jakob (1997) 'How users read on the web'. Nielsen Norman Group, Fremont (CA). Available at: www.nngroup.com/articles/how-users-read-on-the-web/

O'Hara, Carolyn (2014) 'The right way to present your business case'. *Harvard Business Review*. Available at: https://hbr.org/2014/07/the-right-way-to-present-your-business-case

Orwell, George (1946) 'Politics and the English language'. *Horizon*, 13 (76), 252–65.

Shariat, Jonathan and Savard Saucier, Cynthia (2016) *Tragic Design: The Impact of Bad Product Design and How to Fix It*. O'Reilly Media, Sebastopol (CA).

Strunk, William Jr and White, E.B. (1999) *The Elements of Style*. Pearson, Harlow.

Wachter-Boettcher, Sara (2017) *Technically Wrong: Sexist Apps, Biased Algorithms, and Other Threats of Toxic Tech*. W.W. Norton & Co, London.

Wachter-Boettcher, Sara and Meyer, Eric (2016) *Design for Real Life*. A Book Apart, New York.

INDEX